THE ORB WEAVER

THE
ORB
WEAVER

· POEMS ·

ROBERT FRANCIS

WESLEYAN UNIVERSITY PRESS
Middletown, Connecticut

Library of Congress Catalog Card Number: 60–7255

Manufactured in the United States of America

First printing, January, 1960; Second printing, August, 1961; Third printing, February, 1967

Some of these poems originally appeared in magazines and anthologies and some in a privately printed book *The Face Against the Glass* (1950). Grateful acknowledgment is made to the editors of the following: *Amherst Poets* 1959; *Forum; The Lyric; The New England Galaxy* (Old Sturbridge Inc.); *New Poems by American Poets,* I (1953), II (1957); *Poetry; The Saturday Review; The Transatlantic Review; The Virginia Quarterly Review; Voices;* and *Yankee.* The poem "Come Out into the Sun" appeared originally in *The New Yorker.*

CONTENTS

· I ·

ENCOUNTER

Those who have touched it or been touched by it
Or brushed by something that the vine has brushed,
Or burning it, have stood where the sly smoke
Has touched them—know the meaning of its name.

The leaf is smooth. Its green its innocence.
A clean, unblemished leaf, glossy when young.
A leaf the unobserving might overlook
And the observing find too prosperous.

I've seen a vine of it so old and crooked
It held a hen-coop in its grip, the stalk
Thick as a man's wrist. There it had grown,
Half out of sight, permitted, undisturbed.

Strangers to it, who on an autumn road
Have found a vine that swept a tree like fire
And gathered it barehanded and brought it home
For color, seldom gathered it again.

Some are immune and some have thought they were
And some, ever so cautiously with gloves,
Finding that it grew too near their homes,
Have tried to root it out and have succeeded

Except that something from the vine fastened
Upon their flesh and burned, and in a year
Or two the vine itself was there again,
Glossy and green and smooth and innocent.

My neighbor's cow grazing beside the road
Munches with joy (and almost with a smile)
The salad of its leaves, transmuting them
Into sweet milk that I will drink tomorrow.

3

BOY RIDING FORWARD BACKWARD

Presto, pronto! Two boys, two horses.
But the boy on backward riding forward
Is the boy to watch.

He rides the forward horse and laughs
In the face of the forward boy on the backward
Horse, and *he* laughs

Back and the horses laugh. They gallop.
The trick is the cool barefaced pretense
There is no trick.

They might be flying, face to face,
On a fast train. They might be whitecaps
Hot-cool-headed,

One curling backward, one curving forward,
Racing a rivalry of waves.
They might, they might—

Across a blue of lake, through trees,
And half a mile away I caught them:
Two boys, two horses.

Through trees and through binoculars
Sweeping for birds. Oh, they were birds
All right, all right.

Swallows that weave and wave and sweep
And skim and swoop and skitter until
The last trees take them.

RITUAL

Night comes no wilier inch-wise step-wise
shadow by shadow, tree by tree
than at the edge of night, single
and with exquisite circumspection
the ruffed grouse.

She has evaded, O how she
evades, the wildfire fox, the hound,
the sun's betrayal and the moon's
cold machinations.

Masked and peripheral she waits,
tingling with intimation, for one
more overtone of darkness against
her ritual supper on the snow—
the small gold maize.

CATCH

Two boys uncoached are tossing a poem together,
Overhand, underhand, backhand, sleight of hand, every hand,
Teasing with attitudes, latitudes, interludes, altitudes,
High, make him fly off the ground for it, low, make him stoop,
Make him scoop it up, make him as-almost-as-possible miss it,
Fast, let him sting from it, now, now fool him slowly,
Anything, everything tricky, risky, nonchalant,
Anything under the sun to outwit the prosy,
Over the tree and the long sweet cadence down,
Over his head, make him scramble to pick up the meaning,
And now, like a posy, a pretty one plump in his hands.

THE BASE STEALER

Poised between going on and back, pulled
Both ways taut like a tightrope-walker,
Fingertips pointing the opposites,
Now bouncing tiptoe like a dropped ball
Or a kid skipping rope, come on, come on,
Running a scattering of steps sidewise,
How he teeters, skitters, tingles, teases,
Taunts them, hovers like an ecstatic bird,
He's only flirting, crowd him, crowd him,
Delicate, delicate, delicate, delicate—now!

PITCHER

His art is eccentricity, his aim
How not to hit the mark he seems to aim **at,**

His passion how to avoid the obvious,
His technique how to vary the avoidance.

The others throw to be comprehended. He
Throws to be a moment misunderstood

Yet not too much. Not errant, arrant, wild,
But every seeming aberration willed.

Not to, yet still, still to communicate
Making the batter understand too late.

TWO WRESTLERS

Two bronzes, but they were passing bronze before
The sculptor

All glint, all gleaming, face to face and grace
To grace

Balanced almost beyond their balance, tingling
To spring—

Who ever saw so point-by-point, so perfect
A pair

That either one—or both—or neither one—
Could win?

If this is trickery, the trick is smooth
In truth

One wrestler challenging—oh how unsafe—
Himself.

THE ROCK CLIMBERS

In this soft age, in my soft
middle age, the rock climbers

Who giving all to love
embrace cold cliffs

Or with spread-eagle arms
enact a crucifixion

Hanging between the **falling**
and the not-attaining

Observed or unobserved
by hawks and vultures—

How vaulting a humility
superb a supererogation

Craggy to break the mind
on and to cool the mind.

APPLE PEELER

Why the unbroken spiral, Virtuoso,
Like a trick sonnet in one long, versatile sentence?

Is it a pastime merely, this perfection,
For an old man, sharp knife, long night, long winter?

Or do your careful fingers move at the stir
Of unadmitted immemorial magic?

Solitaire. The ticking clock. The apple
Turning, turning as the round earth turns.

THE SEED EATERS

The seed eaters, the vegetarian birds,
Redpolls, grosbeaks, crossbills, finches, siskins,
Fly south to winter in our north, so making
A sort of Florida of our best blizzards.

Weed seeds and seeds of pine cones are their pillage,
Alder and birch catkins, such vegetable
Odds and ends as the winged keys of maple
As well as roadside sumac, red-plush-seeded.

Hi! with a bounce in snowflake flocks come juncos
As if a hand had flipped them and tree sparrows,
Now nip and tuck and playing tag, now squatting
All weather-proofed and feather-fluffed on snow.

Hard fare, full feast, I'll say, deep cold, high spirits.
Here's Christmas to Candlemas on a bunting's budget.
From this old seed eater with his beans, his soybeans,
Cracked corn, cracked wheat, peanuts and split peas, hail!

HIGH DIVER

How deep is his duplicity who in a flash
Passes from resting bird to flying bird to fish,

Who momentarily is sculpture, then all motion,
Speed and splash, then climbs again to contemplation.

He is the archer who himself is bow and arrow.
He is the upper-under-world-commuting hero.

His downward going has the air of sacrifice
To some dark seaweed-bearded seagod face to face

Or goddess. Rippling and responsive lies the water
For him to contemplate, then powerfully to enter.

SWIMMER

I

Observe how he negotiates his way
With trust and the least violence, making
The stranger friend, the enemy ally.
The depth that could destroy gently supports him.
With water he defends himself from water.
Danger he leans on, rests in. The drowning sea
Is all he has between himself and drowning.

II

What lover ever lay more mutually
With his beloved, his always-reaching arms
Stroking in smooth and powerful caresses?
Some drown in love as in dark water, and some
By love are strongly held as the green sea
Now holds the swimmer. Indolently he turns
To float.—The swimmer floats, the lover sleeps.

· II ·

SAILBOAT, YOUR SECRET

Sailboat, your secret. With what dove-and-serpent
Craft you trick the old antagonist.
Trick and transpose, snaring him into sponsor.

The blusterer—his blows you twist to blessing.
Your tactics and your tact, O subtle one,
Your war, your peace—you who defer and win.

Not in obeisance, not in defiance you bow,
You bow to him, but in deep irony.
The gull's wing kisses the whitecap not more archly

Than yours. Timeless and motionless I watch
Your craftsmanship, your wiles, O skimmer-schemer,
Your losses to profit, your wayward onwardness.

FLORUIT

Daringly, yet how unerringly
They bring to the cool and nun-like virtues
Of patience or something older than patience,
Silence, absolute silence, and obedience
All the hot virtues of the sun
And being wholly sex are wholly pure.

If with an equal candor we could face
Their unguarded faces, if we could look in silence
Long enough, could we touch finally,
We who when luckiest are said to flower,
Their fiery innocence, their day-long unabashed
Fulfillment, their unregretful falling?

MONADNOCK

If to the taunting peneplain the peak
Is standpat, relic, anachronism,
Fossil, the peak can stand the taunt.

There was a time the peak was not a peak
But granite and resistant core,
Something that refused to wear

Away when time and wind and rivers wore
The rest away. Here is the thing
The nervous rivers left behind.

Endurance is the word, not exaltation.
Two words: endurance, exaltation.
Out of endurance, exaltation.

DEMONSTRATION

With what economy, what indolent control
The hawk lies on the delicate air, looking below.
He does not climb—watch him—he does not need to climb.

The same invisible shaft that lifts the cumulus
Lifts him, lifts him to any altitude he wills.
Never his wings, only his scream, disturbs noon stillness.

Days of the sharp-cut cloud, mid-day, he demonstrates
Over and ever again the spiral. On smooth blue ice
Impeccable the figure-skater carves his curves.

Oh, how to separate (inseparable in the bird)
His altitude from his incessant livelihood:
His higher mathematics, his hunger on the ground.

SUN

Arch-democrat of our enlightenment
More Jeffersonian than Jefferson,
You warm and warn us with your declaration,
You dazzle us noonly with your rights of man.

Impartially and with strict indifference
You span, cross, and belittle rivers and ranges
And every boundary natural and unnatural
And every visible or invisible fence.

Your light—unspeculated in, unhoarded,
Unallocated, unrationed, and untaxed,
Unprocessed, unpackaged, and unsold—affirms
Uneconomic unpolitical fact.

Your being or non-being philosophers
Do not dispute. *You* are your evidence.
And the simple do not have to have revealed
To them, Revealer, your benevolence.

The loved, the unloved, indistinguishably,
Lift to your comprehensive kiss. Where
Could be rival constancy-intensity?
Where else so gentle and so fierce a fire?

O Sun, unbribed, unbribable and pure,
Sun irreproachable, juster and more
Equitable than jury, judge, and court,
You guarantee the basest weed its light.

Under your blaze grass greens and flowers glitter,
The white sheet on the line burns whiter, whiter,
To terra cotta the slow sun-bather tempers
And the pouring water-bather turns pure copper.

THE ALOOF PEAK

Over the level years the peak persuades me
With its aloofness, its cool disinclination
To be too patently in view, on view.

I acquiesce in its long un-unveilings.
Wrapt and rapt in cloak and contemplation
It loses itself, a standing Socrates

For days and days. Or under its boughing Bo
Of cloud, Buddha the time-oblivious.
Only the little sightseer is rebuffed,

Busy and buzzing with his binoculars,
By so much otherworldliness, by so
Uncoy a coyness, so otherwise a wisdom.

Incognito and incommunicado
It broods, while all the subsidiary hills
Camp like disciples at the foot, the feet.

SQUASH IN BLOSSOM

How lush, how loose, the uninhibited squash is.
If ever hearts (and these immoderate leaves
Are vegetable hearts) were worn on sleeves,
The squash's are. In green the squash vine gushes.

The flowers are cornucopias of summer,
Briefly exuberant and cheaply golden.
And if they make a show of being hidden,
Are open promiscuously to every comer.

Let the squash be what it was doomed to be
By the old Gardener with the shrewd green thumb.
Let it expand and sprawl, defenseless, dumb.
But let me be the fiber-disciplined tree

Whose leaf (with something to say in wind) is small,
Reduced to the ingenuity of a green splinter
Sharp to defy or fraternize with winter,
Or if not that, prepared in fall to fall.

TOMATOES

Nature and God by some elusive yet felicitous
Division of labor that I do not comprehend
(Salts of the soil, rain, the exuberant August sun,
Omniscience, omnipresence, and omnipotence)
Contrived these gaudy fruits, but I was the gardener
And in their lustihood, their hot vermilion luster,
Their unassailable three-dimensionality,
Their unashamed fatness, share the glory and fulfillment.

Now while the sacrificial knife is in abeyance
They bask and blaze serenely on the sun-splashed sill
For the last perfection of ripeness. A thank offering.
A peace offering. A still life. So still, so lifelike
The fruit becomes the painted picture of the fruit.

WAXWINGS

Four Tao philosophers as cedar waxwings
chat on a February berrybush
in sun, and I am one.

Such merriment and such sobriety—
the small wild fruit on the tall stalk—
was this not always my true style?

Above an elegance of snow, beneath
a silk-blue sky a brotherhood of four
birds. Can you mistake us?

To sun, to feast, and to converse
and all together—for this I have abandoned
all my other lives.

REMIND ME OF APPLES

When the cicada celebrates the heat,
Intoning that tomorrow and today
Are only yesterday with the same dust
To dust on plantain and on roadside yarrow—
Remind me, someone, of the apples coming,
Cold in the dew of deep October grass,
A prophecy of snow in their white flesh.

In the long haze of dog days, or by night
When thunder growls and prowls but will not go
Or come, I lose the memory of apples.
Name me the names, the Goldens, Russets, Sweets,
Pippin and Blue Pearmain and Seek-no-further
And the lost apples on forgotten farms
And the wild pasture apples of no name.

GOLD

Suddenly all the gold I ever wanted
Let loose and fell on me. A storm of gold
Starting with rain a quick sun catches falling
And in the rain (fall within fall) a whirl
Of yellow leaves, glitter of paper nuggets.

And there were puddles the sun was winking at
And fountains saucy with goldfish, fantails, sunfish,
And trout slipping in streams it would be insult
To call gold and, trailing their incandescent
Fingers, meteors and a swimming moon.

Flowers of course. Chrysanthemums and clouds
Of twisted cool witch-hazel and marigolds,
Late dandelions and all the goldenrods.
And bees all pollen and honey, wasps gold-banded
And hornets dangling their legs, cruising the sun.

The luminous birds, goldfinches and orioles,
Were gone or going, leaving some of their gold
Behind in near-gold, off-gold, ultra-golden
Beeches, birches, maples, apples. And under
The appletrees the lost, the long-lost names.

Pumpkins and squashes heaped in a cold-gold sunset—
Oh, I was crushed like Croesus, Midas-smothered
And I died in a maple-fall a boy was raking
Nightward to burst all bonfire-gold together—
And leave at last in a thin blue prayer of smoke.

FARM BOY AFTER SUMMER

A seated statue of himself he seems.
A bronze slowness becomes him. Patently
The page he contemplates he doesn't see.

The lesson, the long lesson, has been summer.
His mind holds summer as his skin holds sun.
For once the homework, all of it, was done.

What were the crops, where were the fiery fields
Where for so many days so many hours
The sun assaulted him with glittering showers?

Expect a certain absence in his presence.
Expect all winter long a summer scholar,
For scarcely all its snows can cool that color.

· III ·

EXCLUSIVE BLUE

Her flowers were exclusive blue.
No other color scheme would do.

Better than God she could reject
Being a gardener more select.

Blue, blue it was against the green
With nothing *not* blue sown or seen.

Yet secretly she half-confessed
With blue she was not wholly blessed.

All blues, she found, do not agree.
Blue riots in variety.

Purist-perfectionist at heart,
Her vision flew beyond her art—

Beyond her art, her touch, her power
To teach one blue to each blue flower.

BEYOND BIOLOGY

Teased and titillated by the need
Always of something more than necessary,
Some by-product beyond biology,
The poet is like a boy poised on a rock
Who must produce an original waterfall,
Father a brook, or fertilize a tree.
Remember how young Gulliver quenched the fire?
Pure boy. Pure poet. The Lilliputian palace
Was saved, the emperor grateful, but the empress
(How like an empress) was implacably shocked.

THE REVELERS *

Hill after bumpkin hill blinking
wakes and wildweeds startle into flowers,
flowers into stars
unfrivolously winking
as fat ambassadorial bees
buzz in and out of embassies.

Tailored in moss-green satin
an old man indisputably of the old school,
silent in Latin,
perambulates the unruffled street
as if to demonstrate
paradigms of cool.

Then three young bucks, daisies above their ears,
bare-armed, bare-headed, breeze along
whistling as a glee to the god of weather
like a wind trio, in parts, a three-part song,
mobbed by envious and incredulous birds
in a musical dither.

Maples and elms bystanding laugh
a light leaf
to hear the wisecrack of a gun
from some inspired rapscallion.
Ceremonially a brick battalion
of chimneys salute the sun.

Hornpipes and hymns in mixed musicology,
Verdi from a green musicbox,
a fiddle hilarious with one string,
a deaconess with a sudden rage to sing

* A poem commissioned jointly by the Foundation for Innocence in
the Arts and the Fund for the Advancement of Joy.

the doxology—
not to mention musical clocks.

In pure voluptuousness people take off their shoes
to test the felicity of grass,
the luxury of lawns.
Dark girls turn dryad without trying
and boys of a certain cast impersonate fauns
and even try flying.

Infants with the gift of speech
talk to the larger flowers and, bending, listen.
One chick is filling a fluted squashblossom
for cornucopia with dewberries,
lowbush blueberries,
and all the red raspberries within reach.

And when the churchbells, firebells, cry noon,
picnics fit for an Eighteenth-Century picture,
buttermilk to overflowing,
dew-cold, butter-flecked and thick
enough to eat with a spoon,
and salads, salads that won't stop growing.

Wherever fountains, pools, puddles, or hoses
spill, urchins and nymphs undress
to their last pink roses
to put on glass or better than glass
beads of water
or something wetter.

And poets as guilelessly as running
boys catch butterflies in nets
catch butterflies and better than butterflies in verses

and, staking their virtuosity in punning,
open plump metaphorical purses
and make tall bets.

But one at an oriel, brooding and dreamy,
folds his poem-to-love in the form of a kite
or glider and, leaning, lets it go
down through the zigzag air, and so
(and so easily)
publishes it by giving it flight.

Elsewhere old Mrs. Goldthwaite wishing the unusual
touch to her herb tea,
flies to the hornet attic and comes down,
just as tinkling callers call,
in her (seacaptain's wife) grandmother's receiving gown
of cool pongee.

Mint, Mrs. Edelweiss, sage, or camomile?
Mint, please. Glory, how your teaspoons shine!
Purring Mrs. Goldthwaite pours. Meanwhile
old Mr. Goldthwaite puttering down cellar,
unmindful of any caller,
unearths a bottle of old elderflower wine.

The teadrinkers indoors hear the outdoor dancers
in shadows blue, shadows oblique,
dancers whose figurations open and close
like questions and answers.
Jack picks a daisy, dancing, with his toes
and little kids play hide-and-seek.

Till under the solemn moon they all turn silly
trying to catch the white milk in their hands

to spatter one another's faces,
running impossible races,
hunting the red tigerlily,
discovering undiscoverable lands.

But the moon, the moon stays sober and reaches
down, after a time, to touch them
coolly in white-curtained rooms—
the old like gothic carvings on old tombs,
the children not so much sleeping as enchanted
seashells on remote beaches.

COME OUT INTO THE SUN

Come out into the sun and bathe your eyes
In undiluted light. On the old brass
Of winter-tarnished grass,
Under these few bronze leaves of oak
Suspended, and a blue ghost of chimney smoke
Sit and grow wise
And empty as a simpleton.

The meadow mouse twitching her nose in prayer
Sniffs at a sunbeam like celestial cheese.
Come out, come out into the sun
And bask your knees
And be an acolyte of the illumined air.
The weathercock who yesterday was cold
Today sings hallelujah hymns in gold.

Soon the small snake will slip her skin
And the gray moth in an old ritual
Unseal her silk cocoon.
Come shed, shed now, your winter-varnished shell
In the deep diathermy of high noon.
The sun, the sun, come out into the sun,
Into the sun, come out, come in.

HALLELUJAH: A SESTINA

A wind's word, the Hebrew Hallelujah.
I wonder they never give it to a boy
(Hal for short) boy with wind-wild hair.
It means Praise God, as well it should since praise
Is what God's for. Why didn't they call my father
Hallelujah instead of Ebenezer?

Eben, of course, but christened Ebenezer,
Product of Nova Scotia (hallelujah).
Daniel, a country doctor, was his father
And my father his tenth and final boy.
A baby and last, he had a baby's praise:
Red petticoat, red cheeks, and crow-black hair.

A boy has little say about his hair
And little about a name like Ebenezer
Except that he can shorten either. Praise
God for that, for that shout Hallelujah.
Shout Hallelujah for everything a boy
Can be that is not his father or grandfather.

But then, before you know it, he is a father
Too and passing on his brand of hair
To one more perfectly defenseless boy,
Dubbing him John or James or Ebenezer
But never, so far as I know, Hallelujah,
As if God didn't need quite that much praise.

But what I'm coming to — Could I ever praise
My father half enough for being a father
Who let me be myself? Sing hallelujah.
Preacher he was with a prophet's head of hair
And what but a prophet's name was Ebenezer,
However little I guessed it as a boy?

Outlandish names of course are never a boy's
Choice. And it takes time to learn to praise.
Stone of Help is the meaning of Ebenezer.
Stone of Help—what fitter name for my father?
Always the Stone of Help however his hair
Might graduate from black to Hallelujah.

Such is the old drama of boy and father.
Praise from a grayhead now with thinning hair.
Sing Ebenezer, Robert, sing Hallelujah!

· IV ·

CYPRESSES

At noon they talk of evening and at evening
Of night, but what they say at night
Is a dark secret.

Somebody long ago called them the Trees
Of Death and they have never forgotten.
The name enchants them.

Always an attitude of solitude
To point the paradox of standing
Alone together.

How many years they have been teaching birds
In little schools, by little skills,
How to be shadows.

WITH THE YEAR'S COOLING

With the year's cooling come the colors of fire.
The later-blooming are the warmer flowers
That blaze and smolder in the thinning hours.

Now in the falling of the unfailing year
The quiet-clicking leaves unlatch a door
To those long landscapes we have waited for.

Bitter and fragrant hangs the smoke-tinged air
From some abandoned bonfire near or far,
While sterner night burns an intenser star.

CONFESSION

Whose every motion floats and flows
Undancing still the dancer dances
And dances in repose.

Heedless the poet drops a spark
On the most casual postal card
That burns a telltale mark.

In vain the lover wears a mask,
In vain denies, confessing more
Than the inquisitive ask.

GLASS

Words of a poem should be glass
But glass so simple-subtle its shape
Is nothing but the shape of what it holds.

A glass spun for itself is empty,
Brittle, at best Venetian trinket.
Embossed glass hides the poem or its absence.

Words should be looked through, should be windows.
The best word were invisible.
The poem is the thing the poet thinks.

If the impossible were not
And if the glass, only the glass,
Could be removed, the poem would remain.

HIDE–AND–SEEK

Here where the dead lie hidden
Too well ever to speak,
Three children unforbidden
Are playing hide-and-seek.

What if for such a hiding
These stones were not designed?
The dead are far from chiding;
The living need not mind.

Too soon the stones that hid them
Anonymously in play
Will learn their names and bid them
Come back to hide to stay.

BLUE JAY

So bandit-eyed, so undovelike a bird
to be my pastoral father's favorite—
skulker and blusterer
whose every arrival is a raid.

Love made the bird no gentler
nor him who loved less gentle.
Still, still the wild blue feather
brings my mild father.

DRY POINT

The undesigning yet designing snow
Lacking the art to rearrange, selects,
Selects nevertheless how artfully
Which of the little brittle winter bushes
And tall dry grasses it will delineate
And which conceal—the more selectively
The deeper the snow, the more effectively.
Oh, what a fine fastidious half-art.
Who would ask paint for it and not all dry point—
The burred accurate line—pure line, pure tone?

THREE DARKS COME DOWN TOGETHER

Three darks come down together,
Three darks close in around me:
Day dark, year dark, dark weather.

They whisper and conspire,
They search me and they sound me
Hugging my private fire.

Day done, year done, storm blowing,
Three darknesses impound me
With dark of white snow snowing.

Three darks gang up to end me,
To browbeat and dumbfound me.
Three future lights defend me.

· **V** ·

PAST TENSE

Cool, rain-gray, classic, thin, the carved slate
Leans a little with age in two directions
But burdens not the dead with needless weight.

There was a time when death was satisfied
With small memento, such as a man could raise
Himself, if he wanted to, before he died—

With delicate willow and (without misgiving)
A verse of his own choosing, elegantly
Misspelled, to offer solace to the living.

Eighteen Hundred. I prefer past tense
In death—these few dark stones within a one-
Time white, long-unrepainted picket fence,

And three or four tall wind-torn wind-defying
Pines, and through the pines one smoke-blue hill
To give perspective to the fact of dying.

BURIAL

Aloft, lightly on fingertips
As crewmen carry a racing shell—
But I was lighter than any shell or ship.

An easy trophy, they picked me up and bore me,
Four of them, an even four.
I knew the pulse and impulse of those hands,

And heard the talking, laughing. I heard
As from an adjoining room, the door ajar,
Voices but not words.

If I am dead (I said)
If this is death,
How casual, how delicate its masque and myth.

One pall bearer, the tenor, spoke,
Another whistled softly, and I tried to smile.
Death? Music? Or a joke?

But still the hands were there.
I rode half on the hands and half in air.
Their strength was equal to my strangeness.

Whatever they do (I said) will be done right,
Whether in earth and dark or in deep light,
Whatever the hands do will be well.

Suddenly I tried to breathe and cry:
Before you put me down, before
I finally die,

Take from the filing folders of my brain
All that is finished or begun—
Then I remembered that this had been done.

So we went on, on
To our party-parting on the hill
Of the blue breath, gray boulder, and my burial.

DESIRING TO GIVE ALL

Desiring to give all, to be all gift,
A living giver, then a giver dead,
He gave to friends the liveliness of his head,
Then stretching generosity with thrift,
Pondered if head itself, the clean bare skull,
Might not be saved and deeded to a friend
So that memorial and functional
Might thrive and blend
In an undying fate
As doorstop or as paper-weight.

EPITAPH

Believer he and unbeliever both
For less than both would have been less than truth.
His creed was godliness and godlessness.
His credit had been cramped with any less.

Freedom he loved and order he embraced.
Fifty extremists called him Janus-faced.
Though cool centrality was his desire,
He drew the zealot fire and counter-fire.

Baffled by what he deeply understood,
He found life evil and he found life good.
Lover he was, unlonely, yet alone—
Esteemed, belittled, nicknamed, and unknown.

THE ORB WEAVER

Here is the spinner, the orb weaver,
Devised of jet, embossed with sulphur,
Hanging among the fruits of summer,

Hour after hour serenely sullen,
Ripening as September ripens,
Plumping like a grape or melon.

And in its winding-sheet the grasshopper.

The art, the craftsmanship, the cunning,
The patience, the self-control, the waiting,
The sudden dart and the needled poison.

I have no quarrel with the spider
But with the mind or mood that made her
To thrive in nature and in man's nature.

TWO BUMS WALK OUT OF EDEN

Two bums walk out of Eden. Evening approaches
The suave, the decorous trees, the careful grass,
The strict green benches—and the two bums go.

They caught the official nod, the backward-pointing
Thumb, and now they rise and leave a little
Briskly as men heedful to waste no time—

As men bending their steps toward due appointments.
The tall one looms like a skeleton; the runt
Walks with the totter of a tumbleweed.

Down the trimmed ceremonial path they go
Together, silent and separate and eyes
Ahead like soldiers. Down the long path and out.

What desert blanched these faces? What blowing sands
Gullied the eyes and scarred the hanging hands
While Babylon and Nineveh were falling?

Now a shade darker will be a shade less dark.
Now there is room for evening in the park
Where cool episcopal bells will soon be calling.

DOG-DAY NIGHT

Just before night darkens to total night
A child at the next farm is calling, calling,
Calling her dog. Heat and the death of wind
Bring the small wailing like a mosquito close.
Will nothing stop her? Yet my complaining adds
To my complaint. Welcome it like a bird,
A whippoorwill, I say, closing my windows
North and east. The voice evades the glass.
She will not, will not let the dog be lost.
Why don't they tell her, isn't she old enough
To hear how the whole dog-gone earth is loose
And snooping through the dark and won't come home?

COLD

Cold and the colors of cold: mineral, shell,
And burning blue. The sky is on fire with blue
And wind keeps ringing, ringing the fire bell.

I am caught up into a chill as high
As creaking glaciers and powder-plumed peaks
And the absolutes of interstellar sky.

Abstract, impersonal, metaphysical, pure,
This dazzling art derides me. How should warm breath
Dare to exist—exist, exult, endure?

Hums in my ear the old Ur-father of freeze
And burn, that pre-post-Christian Fellow before
And after all myths and demonologies.

Under the glaring and sardonic sun,
Behind the icicles and double glass
I huddle, hoard, hold out, hold on, hold on.

THE DISENGAGING EAGLE

There is a rumor
>the eagle tires of being eagle
and would change wing
with a less kingly bird as king,
say, the seagull.

>With swans and cranes and geese,
so the rumor goes,
finding his official pose
faintly absurd,
he would aspire to unofficial peace
and be, if possible, pure bird.

There is a rumor
>the eagle nurses now a mood
to abdicate
forever and for good
as flagpole-sitter for the State.

>Is it the fall of age
merely, a geriatrical complaint,
this drift to disengage,
this cool unrage?
or rather some dark philosophic taint?

There is a rumor
>(God save us) the old warrior
who screamed against the sun
and toured with Caesar and Napoleon
cavils now at war

>and would allegedly retire,
resign, retreat
to a blue solitude,

an inaccessible country seat
to fan a native fire,
a purely personal feud.